Look Who's Reading!

a *Collections for Young Scholars*™ book

OPEN COURT PUBLISHING COMPANY

CHICAGO AND PERU, ILLINOIS

PROGRAM AUTHORS
Marilyn Jager Adams
Carl Bereiter
Jan Hirshberg
Valerie Anderson
S. A. Bernier

CONSULTING AUTHORS
Michael Pressley
Iva Carruthers
Bill Pinkney

CHAIRMAN
M. Blouke Carus

PRESIDENT
André W. Carus

EDUCATION DIRECTOR
Carl Bereiter

CONCEPT
Barbara Conteh

EXECUTIVE EDITORS
Nancy Dyer
Shirley Graudin

SENIOR PROJECT EDITOR
Nancy Johnson

ART DIRECTOR
John Grandits

VICE-PRESIDENT, PRODUCTION
AND MANUFACTURING
Chris Vancalbergh

PERMISSIONS COORDINATOR
Diane Sikora

COVER ARTIST
Hilary Knight

ACKNOWLEDGMENTS

Grateful acknowledgment is given to the following publishers and copyright owners for permission granted to reprint selections from their publications. All possible care has been taken to trace ownership and secure permission for each selection included.

Curtis Brown, Ltd.: "Babybuggy" by Jane Yolen, copyright © 1991 by Jane Yolen.

National Wildlife Federation: "If I Were a Mouse" by Solveig Paulson Russell from the September Series III issue of *Your Big Backyard* magazine, copyright © 1984 by the National Wildlife Federation.

The Society of Authors, as the literary representative of the Estate of Rose Fyleman, and Pamela Sweet: "What They Said," translated by Rose Fyleman, art by Pamela Sweet, illustrations copyright © 1991 by Pamela Sweet.

CONTENTS

LAUGHING SONG

William Blake

illustrated by Susannah Ryan

Come live and be merry,
and join with me,
To sing the sweet chorus
of "Ha, ha, he!"

FINE ART
LOOK WHO'S READING!

Layla and Majnun at School.
1524–1525. Artist unknown,
style of Shaykh Zadeh.

The Libraries Are Appreciated.
1943. Jacob Lawrence.

Untitled. c. 1989. Keith Haring.

THE PURPLE COW

Gelett Burgess

illustrated by Luis de Horna

I never saw a Purple Cow,

I never hope to see one;

But I can tell you, anyhow,
I'd rather see than be one!

HEY, DIDDLE, DIDDLE

illustrated by Bonnie MacKain

Hey, diddle, diddle!

The cat and the fiddle,

The cow jumped over the moon;

The little dog laughed

To see such sport,

And the dish ran away with the spoon.

Cheering

Reading

Playing

Listening

Kicking

Running

Feeding

Eating

Building

Digging

10

WHAT THEY SAID

German Nursery Rhyme
translated by Rose Fyleman
illustrated by Pamela Sweet

"It's four o'clock,"
said the

cock

"It's still dark,"
said the

lark

🐛 12

"What's that?"
said the

cat

"I want to sleep,"
said the

sheep

"A bad habit,"
said the

rabbit

"Of course,"
said the

horse

"Let's have a spree,"
said the

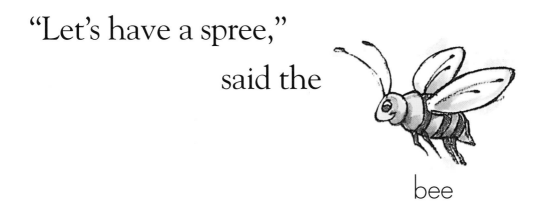

bee

"But where?"
said the

hare

"In the barrow," said the

sparrow

"I'm too big," said the

pig

"In the  ,"

house

said the

mouse

But the

said,

dog

"Bow-wow, it's too late now."

17

RAIN

Robert Louis Stevenson

illustrated by Ed Miller

The rain is raining all around,
It falls on field and tree,
It rains on the umbrellas here,
And on the ships at sea.

IF I WERE A MOUSE

Solveig Paulson Russell

photograph by
Alvin E. Staffan

If I were a mouse,

a mouse, a mouse,

I'd never live in

a house, a house;

I'd live outside

where grass

grows tall,

With other

mouse friends,

big and small.

TINGALAYO

from The Second Raffi Songbook

illustrated by Doug Cushman

Tingalayo come little donkey come.

Tingalayo come little donkey come.

Me donkey fast,

me donkey slow,

Me donkey come and me donkey go.

21

Me donkey hee, me donkey haw,
Me donkey sleep in a bed of straw.

Me donkey dance, me donkey sing,
Me donkey wearin' a diamond ring.

Me donkey swim,

me donkey ski,

Me donkey dress elegantly.

Tingalayo come little donkey come.

Tingalayo come little donkey come.

BABYBUGGY

Jane Yolen

illustrated by Rex Schneider

Ladybuggy's
babybuggy
rides inside
a buggysnuggie.

When he cries,
Ms. Ladybuggy
gives him a big
buggyhuggy.

Drinking from a
buggymuggy,
lying on a buggyruggy,

bathing in a buggytubby,
wait—don't pull the
buggypluggy!
Silly baby ladybuggy.

THE HOUSE THAT JACK BUILT

English Nursery Rhyme

illustrated by Randolph Caldecott

This is the House that Jack built.

This is the Malt,
That lay in the House
    that Jack built.

This is the Rat,
That ate the Malt,
That lay in the House
    that Jack built.

This is the Cat,
That killed the Rat,
That ate the Malt,
That lay in the House
     that Jack built.

This is the Dog,
That worried the Cat,
That killed the Rat,
That ate the Malt,
That lay in the House
        that Jack built.

This is the Cow
     with the crumpled horn,
That tossed the Dog,
That worried the Cat,
That killed the Rat,
That ate the Malt,
That lay in the House
     that Jack built.

This is the Maiden all forlorn,
That milked the Cow
   with the crumpled horn,
That tossed the Dog,
That worried the Cat,
That killed the Rat,
That ate the Malt,
That lay in the House
   that Jack built.

This is the Man all tattered and torn,

That kissed the Maiden all forlorn,

That milked the Cow
    with the crumpled horn,

That tossed the Dog,

That worried the Cat,

That killed the Rat,

That ate the Malt,

That lay in the House
    that Jack built.